# Extreme Places
# The Hottest and the Coldest

### KATIE MARSICO

**Children's Press®**
An Imprint of Scholastic Inc.

**Content Consultant**
Injeong Jo, PhD
Assistant Professor
Department of Geography
Texas State University
San Marcos, Texas

Library of Congress Cataloging-in-Publication Data
Marsico, Katie, 1980– author.
The hottest and the coldest / by Katie Marsico.
    pages cm. — (A true book)
 Summary: "Learn all about the hottest and coldest places on Earth and find out what it takes for
life to survive in these extreme locations"— Provided by publisher.
 Includes bibliographical references and index.
 ISBN 978-0-531-21844-0 (library binding) — ISBN 978-0-531-21783-2 (pbk.)
 1. Climatic extremes—Juvenile literature. 2. Dhahran (Saudi Arabia)—Climate—Juvenile literature.
 3. Antarctica—Climate—Juvenile literature. I. Title. II. Series: True book.
 QC981.8.C53M37 2016
 551.6'2—dc23                                                    2015007187

All rights reserved. Published in 2016 by Children's Press, an imprint of Scholastic Inc.
Printed in the United States of America 113
SCHOLASTIC, CHILDREN'S PRESS, A TRUE BOOK™, and associated logos are trademarks and/or
registered trademarks of Scholastic Inc.
1 2 3 4 5 6 7 8 9 10 R 25 24 23 22 21 20 19 18 17 16

**Front cover (main): A climber entering a glacier cave in Alaska**

**Front cover (inset): Ecuador's Tungurahua Volcano erupting**

**Back cover: A sign in Death Valley warning visitors of extreme heat**

# Find the Truth!

**Everything** you are about to read is true *except* for one of the sentences on this page.

Which one is **TRUE**?

**T or F**   Humidity adds to the extreme heat in Saudi Arabia.

**T or F**   Most glacier caves last for centuries.

Find the answers in this book.

# Contents

THE **BIG** TRUTH!

**Insulated jacket**

A vent deep in the Atlantic Ocean shoots out hot water and minerals.

Few explorers have journeyed inside U.S. glacier caves.

Desert temperatures rise quickly at sunrise and drop quickly after sunset.

# From Blistering Heat to Bitter Cold

In Dhahran, Saudi Arabia, children play in their air-conditioned living room. The afternoon sun blazes outside. Once the sun starts to set, the children will head to the park. Meanwhile, it is best to keep cool. In Dhahran, the daytime **heat index** sometimes climbs to 176 degrees Fahrenheit (80 degrees Celsius)! It is a blistering example of one of Earth's temperature extremes. Such extremes shape life for people and countless other organisms.

# Different Examples of Extremes

Of course, temperature extremes are not always about heat. People, plants, animals, and other organisms have also **adapted,** or adjusted, to extreme cold. For instance, in portions of Antarctica, the **wind chill** makes it feel as frigid as –134°F (–92°C)!

Temperature extremes also occur in more unexpected locations. Sometimes, extremes shape life far beneath the surface of the ocean. In other cases, they create the conditions for ice caves hidden within glaciers.

**People need special clothing and other gear to brave the cold in Antarctica.**

Temperature affects precipitation. Precipitation tends to fall as rain when temperatures are warmer, and snow develops when temperatures are colder.

To understand temperature extremes, it is important to know exactly what temperature is and how it is measured. Temperature is how hot or cold an object or substance is. Air temperature influences weather. Weather describes the state of the air surrounding Earth. This includes wind, clouds, precipitation, and other natural activity in the atmosphere.

The Fahrenheit scale was introduced in 1724. Celsius was introduced in 1742.

## More About Measuring Temperature

Temperature is typically measured on one of two scales: Fahrenheit or Celsius. Using the Fahrenheit scale, water freezes at 32°F and boils at 212°F. On the Celsius scale, water freezes at 0°C and boils at 100°C. Fahrenheit is often used in the United States. The Celsius scale is used by scientists and by people who live in most other countries.

Wind chill and heat index both affect temperatures. Wind chill is the temperature someone feels as a result of wind speed combined with the actual air temperature. The heat index is the temperature a person experiences because of **relative humidity** and actual air temperature.

To survive, all living things must adapt to the temperatures within their environment. Humans, through their exceptional ability to adapt, are in a unique position to experience and study the ways that temperature extremes shape the world.

People have found many ways to cool down when it is hot outside, including fans and air-conditioning.

Areas of Saudi Arabia along the Persian Gulf tend to be much more humid than the rest of the country.

# Saudi Arabian Scorcher

In Dhahran, Saudi Arabia, scorching heat is not always the norm. In fact, in winter, average daily heat indices tend to fall to between 58° and 67°F (14° and 19°C). Yet summers are a different story. Hot air temperatures combine with intense humidity created by the nearby Persian Gulf. The result is summer heat indices that often make it feel as hot as 140°F (60°C).

Saudi Arabia borders the Persian Gulf.

Persian Gulf
Dhahran,
Saudi Arabia

# A Risky Record Breaker

On July 8, 2003, a record-breaking temperature extreme occurred in Dhahran. That day, air temperatures soared to 108°F (42°C) and relative humidity was greater than normal. These conditions made it feel like 176°F (80°C). That's the highest heat index ever recorded on Earth! To put this in perspective, that is only 36°F (2°C) cooler than the point at which water boils.

**Children rest under a warm sun in Dhahran.**

Heatstroke symptoms include headache, dizziness and confusion, muscle weakness, and nausea.

With particularly high heat indices, people do not just experience a little sweat and stickiness. At a heat index of more than 130°F (54°C), heatstroke is a serious and immediate risk. Heatstroke occurs when extreme heat causes a person's body temperature to rise to 104°F (40°C) or greater. If untreated, heatstroke can damage the brain, heart, kidneys, and muscles. It can even lead to death.

The nearby Persian Gulf can be a great place to cool off in the heat along Saudi Arabia's gulf coast.

# Beat the Heat!

The heat index in Dhahran has not risen that high since July 2003. Yet residents still have to survive scorching—and sometimes unsafe—summer weather. Fortunately, they have developed methods of coping with the extreme heat.

People in Dhahran often plan meetings and social activities in the morning or early evening. The afternoon, when the sun's rays are the strongest, is the hottest time of day outside.

Many people rely on air-conditioning to stay cool. In this part of the world, people also wear light-colored, loose-fitting clothing that absorbs and traps less heat.

Engineers and city planners have also figured out ways to help Dhahran's residents beat the heat. For example, they frequently place parking lots close to building entrances. This reduces the amount of time someone has to walk outside.

Traditional loose robes called *thawbs* are perfectly suited to Saudi Arabia's hot temperatures.

Antarctica is about 1.4 times the size of the United States.

# CHAPTER 3

# The Frozen Continent

About 8,500 miles (13,679 kilometers) southeast of Saudi Arabia lies another land of dramatic temperature extremes—Antarctica. Ninety-eight percent of the "frozen continent" is covered in ice. Much of that ice measures roughly 7,000 feet (2,133 meters) thick! And in this land of glaciers and blizzards, it gets colder than anywhere else on Earth. The average yearly temperature in Antarctica is −54°F (−48°C).

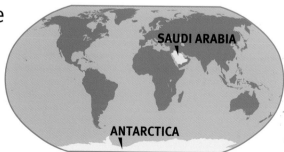

# Constantly Cool

Antarctica is always frozen because it sits at Earth's southernmost point, around the South Pole. Earth is slightly tilted as it orbits the sun. As a result, Earth's poles spend half the year angled toward the sun and the other half angled away. This creates long, dark winters, during which the poles receive little warmth from the sun. Even during the summer, the poles do not face the sun directly and do not receive much heat.

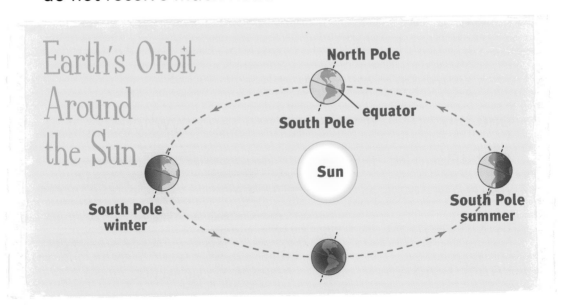

Earth's Orbit Around the Sun

North Pole

South Pole

equator

Sun

South Pole winter

South Pole summer

Antarctica's record low temperature is more than 136 times cooler than many freezers!

Antarctica is made even colder by its snow and ice, which reflect the sun's rays rather than absorbing them. Antarctica's **altitude** is also the highest of any continent. Temperatures tend to be lower at higher altitudes. In addition, winds whip at almost 200 miles (322 km) per hour along Antarctica's coast. Combined with almost no humidity, these conditions make for extremely low temperatures. On August 10, 2010, the East Antarctic **Plateau** experienced Earth's coldest recorded temperature. Wind chill made it feel like −136°F (−93°C).

Researchers in Antarctica study a range of topics, from local wildlife to the world's climate. This researcher is studying penguin eggs.

# Coping With the Cold

Unlike every other continent, Antarctica is not home to **indigenous peoples**. The humans who spend time there are from different countries around the world. Most long-term visitors to the frozen continent are researchers.

People visiting Antarctica must protect themselves from the frigid weather. Otherwise, they would be at great risk of suffering from dangerous conditions such as frostbite and **hypothermia**.

Visitors wear several layers of clothing, including two to three pairs of gloves. Layering prevents the cold from reaching people's skin and helps trap body heat. In extremely frigid areas, people take even more precautions. For example, air surrounding the East Antarctic Plateau is so cold that it is harmful to a person's lungs. Researchers wear a special coat with a snorkel tube. Air is warmed when it passes through the snorkel and into the coat, where it in turn warms the person's body.

**A researcher uses a pick to collect samples of meteorites that landed in Antarctica.**

# Animal Adaptations

Animals have also adapted to Antarctica's extreme temperatures. Several types of whales and seals swim in Antarctic waters. They rely on blubber, a layer of fat beneath their skin, to keep warm. Antarctica's penguins have blubber, too, as well as thick, waterproof feathers.

Being cold and wet typically lowers body temperature more than simply being cold. Waterproof feathers prevent a penguin's skin from becoming soaked when it dives underwater to catch fish. As a result, the bird stays drier—and warmer!

**Antarctica's emperor penguins can dive as deep as 1,850 feet (564 m) into frigid waters that can be as cold as 28°F (–2°C).**

# Where Scientists Stay

Antarctica's research centers are specially suited to long-term stays in extreme conditions. For example, Halley VI Research Station (below) is divided into eight portable units that are all fitted with special legs. The legs can be raised when snow accumulates, or collects, so the station always stays above it. Halley provides scientists with different areas for dining, relaxing, sleeping, lab research, office work, and scientific observation. There are roughly 16 to 70 people residing there at any given time.

# Being Prepared

Preparedness is one of the main ways people have learned to adapt to temperature extremes. Whether dealing with a scorching heat index or subzero wind chill, being ready often makes a life-or-death difference.

### The Right Foods
In extremely cold temperatures, it is important to eat high-calorie foods. These include breads, pastas, and cereals. Such choices provide the extra energy people need to stay warm. Meanwhile, in extreme heat, nonperishable foods that will not spoil quickly are good options.

### Sunscreen and Sunglasses
These items come in handy in both hot and cold weather. Remember that snow and ice reflect the rays of the sun! In addition, goggles are a good line of defense against blowing snow.

## Enough Water

In extreme heat, people sweat more. As they lose more bodily fluid, they run a greater risk of dehydration. In these temperatures, experts recommend drinking 16 to 32 ounces (473 to 946 milliliters) of water an hour. That is about two to four glasses. Dressing in layers, as people do in cold temperatures, often triggers sweating, too. Therefore, people should also drink plenty of water in cold weather.

## Proper Clothing

When extreme heat is predicted, it is helpful to wear loose, light-colored, lightweight clothing. Items made from cotton and linen are often best. For extremely cold temperatures, it is more practical to dress in layers. The outer layer should be made from a material that is both windproof and waterproof.

## Shelter

In extreme heat, people should spend *at least* two hours a day in a sheltered area with air-conditioning. In extreme cold, the ideal shelter features a working furnace and properly insulated windows and doors.

## Emergency Items

Because extreme weather sometimes causes power outages, it is wise to keep a battery-operated flashlight and radio handy. It is also helpful to have a first-aid kit and clean, dry towels and linens.

The water that hydrothermal vents emit is filled with minerals.

# CHAPTER 4

# In Hot Water

Few beachgoers would compare the experience of swimming in the often-chilly Atlantic Ocean with soaking in a hot tub. Yet things are extremely different far beneath the waves—about 1.9 miles (3 km) down, to be exact. At those depths, the water temperature in certain areas reaches a sizzling 867°F (464°C)! How can this be? Hydrothermal vents are the hot-water heaters of the ocean floor.

Atlantic
Ocean

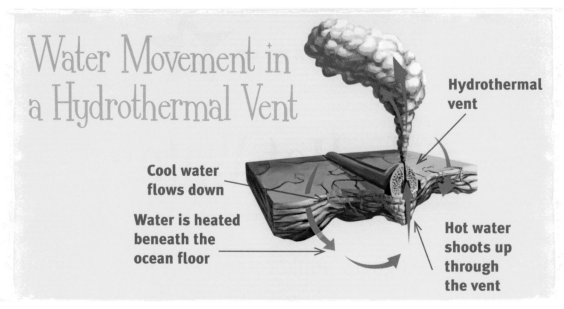

# Water Movement in a Hydrothermal Vent

**Hydrothermal vent**

**Cool water flows down**

**Water is heated beneath the ocean floor**

**Hot water shoots up through the vent**

## Action on the Ocean Floor

Hydrothermal vents are underwater hot springs. They usually occur where the edges of Earth's **tectonic plates** grind together. This opens up cracks in the ocean floor. Friction from the grinding also creates heat, which melts rock to magma. A hydrothermal vent develops when cold seawater filters through the cracks and is heated by the magma beneath.

Hydrothermal vents exist in oceans around the world. Yet scientists believe those in the Atlantic Ocean pump the hottest water on Earth.

The water that comes from hydrothermal vents serves an important purpose. It contains minerals that support life at the bottom of the ocean. Plants and animals closer to the ocean's surface depend on sunlight for energy. More than 10,000 feet (3,048 m) beneath the waves, however, the ocean floor is cloaked in darkness. Tiny organisms living there, such as **phytoplankton**, obtain their energy from minerals in the water.

**Phytoplankton like these thrive in the water around hydrothermal vents.**

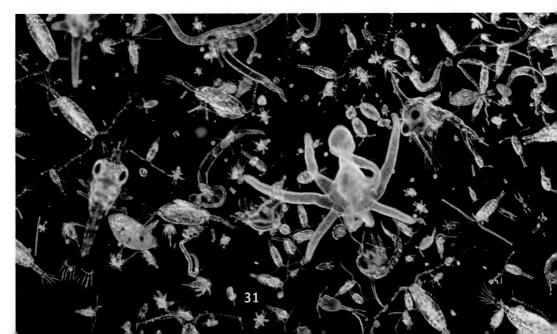

# Not Easy to Explore

Studying hydrothermal vents is not easy. The liquid they produce is nearly four times the boiling point of water. As a result, scientists would be scalded, or burned, if they got too close. In addition, hydrothermal vents are located far below the ocean's surface. Traveling to such depths is often difficult and dangerous.

Basic scuba gear is enough for most divers to go about 130 feet (40 m) underwater. Going deeper requires more specialized equipment.

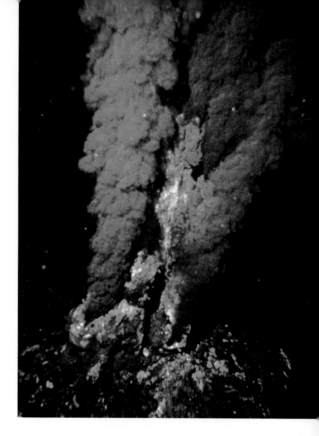

Some of Earth's hottest hydrothermal vents are called black smokers. The name comes from the color of the materials that shoot from the vent.

At the same time, scientists cannot use robotic tools to investigate the vents. The temperature of the water is hot enough to melt drills and other equipment. For now, scientists must rely on computer models to explore vents in the deepest, darkest parts of the Atlantic. They hope these models will continue to provide information about Earth's hottest water and the minerals it contains.

Two people stand at the entrance
of one of Sandy Glacier's caves.

Glaciers cover about
10 percent of Earth's land.

# CHAPTER 5

# Within Walls of Ice

When most people hear the word *glacier*, they probably picture a giant, slow-moving sheet of ice. But that is just a snapshot of the surface. What is the view like *within* a glacier?

Since 2011, that is exactly what scientists at Mount Hood in Oregon have been trying to figure out. Sandy Glacier stretches along Mount Hood's western slope. Within it lies a network of ice caves that shape a mysterious frozen world.

Sandy Glacier, Mount Hood

**Sandy Glacier flows very slowly down the side of Mount Hood.**

# How Frozen Caves Form

Sandy Glacier is an alpine glacier. That is a type of glacier that forms near a mountaintop and slowly flows down into a valley. Normally, caves take shape within such glaciers during warmer weather. Rising temperatures cause portions of the ice to melt into water. The water seeps down through cracks in the glaciers. The cracks gradually widen into larger openings, and caves form.

In most cases, the caves ultimately collapse when the seasons change. They are crushed under the weight of the ice that swells and spreads as soon as temperatures drop.

Yet glacier caves are not always seasonal. When a glacier is thin enough, the caves sometimes last longer. Even as the weather cools, they are not crushed by the weight of the ice. This is the case with the Sandy Glacier caves.

**Partial collapse has left this glacier cave in Austria full of holes.**

# Studying the Sandy Glacier Caves

The chain of frozen caves on Mount Hood measures more than 1 mile (1.6 km) long. It is the United States' largest group of glacier caves outside of Alaska. Unlike most ice caves, Mount Hood's are growing. By studying how the ice melts and these caves grow, scientists learn more about how and why glaciers shrink. One main cause is usually related to climate change. As Earth's average temperature increases, the size of glaciers decreases.

A researcher stands by a frozen waterfall in one of Sandy Glacier's caves.

# Worrisome Warming

The rate at which Earth's glaciers are melting is continually speeding up. Scientists say this is an effect of global climate change. In recent decades, scientists have measured a spike in temperatures caused by increases in certain gases, such as carbon dioxide, in the atmosphere. Many scientists argue that human activities such as clearing forests and burning certain fuels, such as coal and oil, are making global warming worse. Experts also point out that melting glaciers lead to rising sea levels, which cause flooding.

**Visitors need special equipment to navigate Sandy Glacier's Pure Imagination Cave.**

To study the cave chain within Sandy Glacier, scientists must know how to both safely climb a mountain and explore a cave. Their equipment includes ropes, special ice screws, axes, helmets, wetsuits, and flashlights. Scientists enter through a moulin, or hole in the glacier's surface. In the caves, they must be careful. Falling rocks are one hazard. Injuries such as sprained ankles are another. Also, being stuck inside would put a person at great risk of hypothermia.

# Wonders of a Hidden World

Scientists who journey to Mount Hood understand that their exploration is risky. Once inside the caves, however, researchers are rewarded by glimpses of a world that few other people view. Deep within the glacier, the thick ice takes on a blue-green glow. Waterfalls are often frozen in place.

Sandy Glacier's three explored caves are named Pure Imagination, Snow Dragon, and Frozen Minotaur.

Whenever scientists venture inside the caves, they are aware that they are walking through a changing environment. Ultimately, Earth's climate will continue to warm. As a result, the glacier—and the caves—on Mount Hood will disappear. It is impossible to predict exactly when this will occur, though it will likely be within the next decade.

**A researcher uses safety rope near the entrance of Sandy Glacier's Snow Dragon cave.**

A person walks to the water's edge to go fishing along Antarctica's coast.

# Incredible Extremes

The Sandy Glacier caves are but one example of several remarkable situations shaped by extreme temperatures. Whether in Oregon, Saudi Arabia, Antarctica, or the depths of the Atlantic, these extremes are often mysterious. In other cases, they are downright dangerous. Yet, no matter when and where they occur, they are almost always fascinating. So are the incredible ways that people, plants, and animals react and respond to them. ★

Earth's highest recorded heat index: 176°F (80°C)

Heat index at which heatstroke becomes a serious and immediate risk: 130°F (54°C)

Maximum wind speeds along Antarctica's coastal regions: 200 mph (322 kph)

Coldest recorded temperature on Earth: –136°F (–93°C)

Depth of hydrothermal vents on the Atlantic Ocean floor: 1.9 mi. (3 km)

Maximum temperature of water produced by hydrothermal vents: 867°F (464°C)

Length of the chain of caves within Sandy Glacier: More than 1 mi. (1.6 km)

When it is likely that Sandy Glacier will disappear: Within the next 10 years

## Did you find the truth?

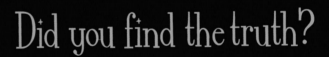

**T** Humidity adds to the extreme heat in Saudi Arabia.

**F** Most glacier caves last for centuries.

# Resources

## Books

Hunter, Nick. *Science vs. Climate Change*. New York: Gareth Stevens Publishing, 2013.

Orr, Tamra B. *Adapting to Severe Heat Waves*. New York: Rosen Central, 2013.

**Visit this Scholastic Web site for more information on hottest and coldest places:**
★ www.factsfornow.scholastic.com
Enter the keywords **Hottest and Coldest**

# Important Words

**adapted** (uh-DAPT-id) — changed over time to fit in better with the environment

**altitude** (AL-ti-tood) — the height of something above the ground or above sea level

**heat index** (HEET IN-deks) — the outside temperature someone feels due to actual air temperature and relative humidity

**hypothermia** (hye-poh-THUHR-mee-uh) — a sometimes fatal condition in which a person's body temperature drops dangerously low

**indigenous peoples** (in-DIH-juh-nuhss PEE-puhlz) — cultures or groups that originated in a particular area

**insulated** (IN-suh-lay-tid) — covered with material in order to stop heat, electricity, or sound from escaping

**phytoplankton** (fye-toh-PLANK-tuhn) — tiny plants that drift or float in water

**plateau** (plah-TOH) — an area of high, flat ground

**relative humidity** (REH-luh-tihv hyoo-MIH-duh-tee) — the amount of water vapor present in the air

**tectonic plates** (tek-TAHN-ik PLAYTS) — huge, rigid sections of rock that make up Earth's crust

**wind chill** (WIND CHILL) — the outside temperature someone feels due to actual air temperature and wind speed

# Index

Page numbers in **bold** indicate illustrations.

# About the Author

Katie Marsico graduated from Northwestern University and worked as an editor in reference publishing before she began writing in 2006. Since that time, she has published more than 200 titles for children and young adults.

Katie enjoyed learning about the wide range of temperature extremes profiled in this book, though she still definitely prefers hot to cold.